Think About Math

Many Birds

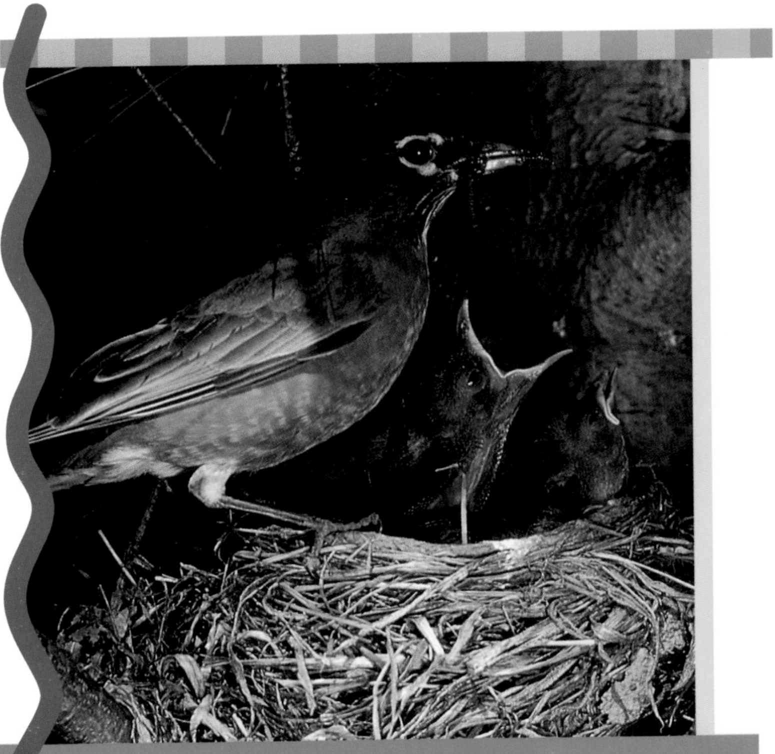

CURRICULUM ASSOCIATES®, Inc.

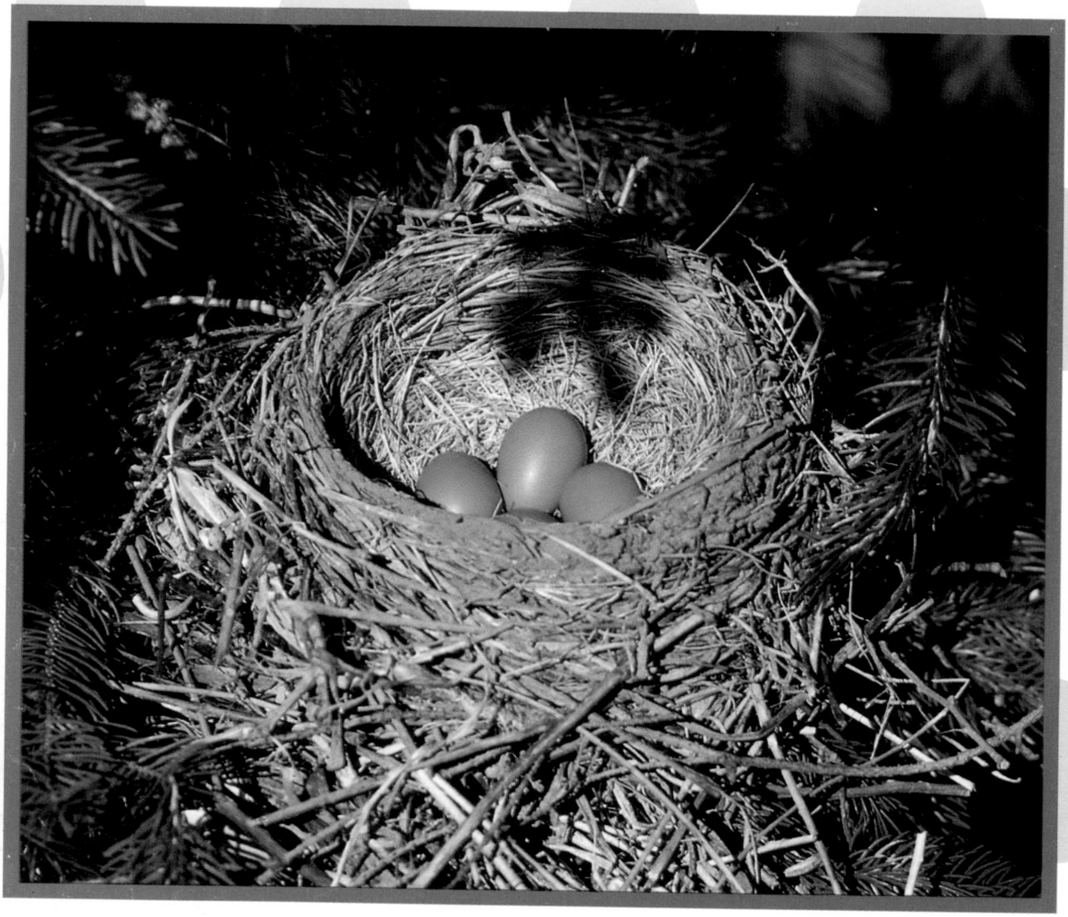

small eggs

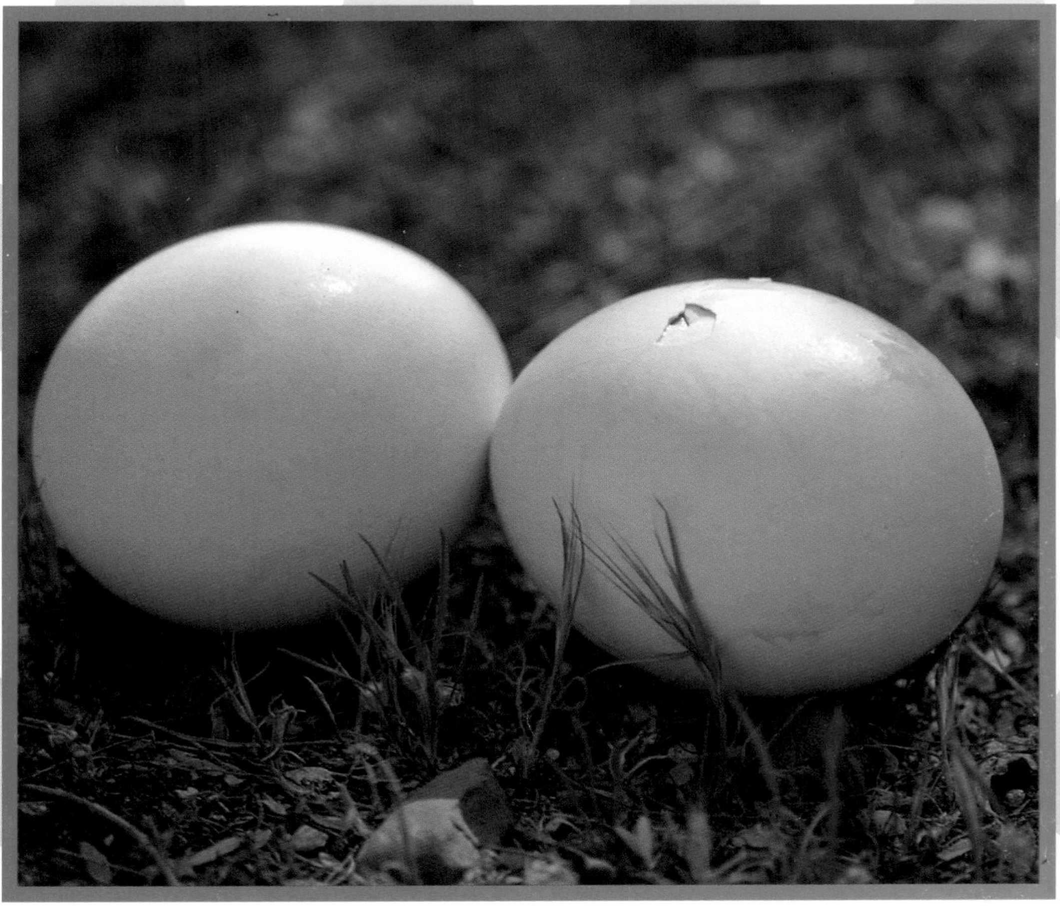

big eggs

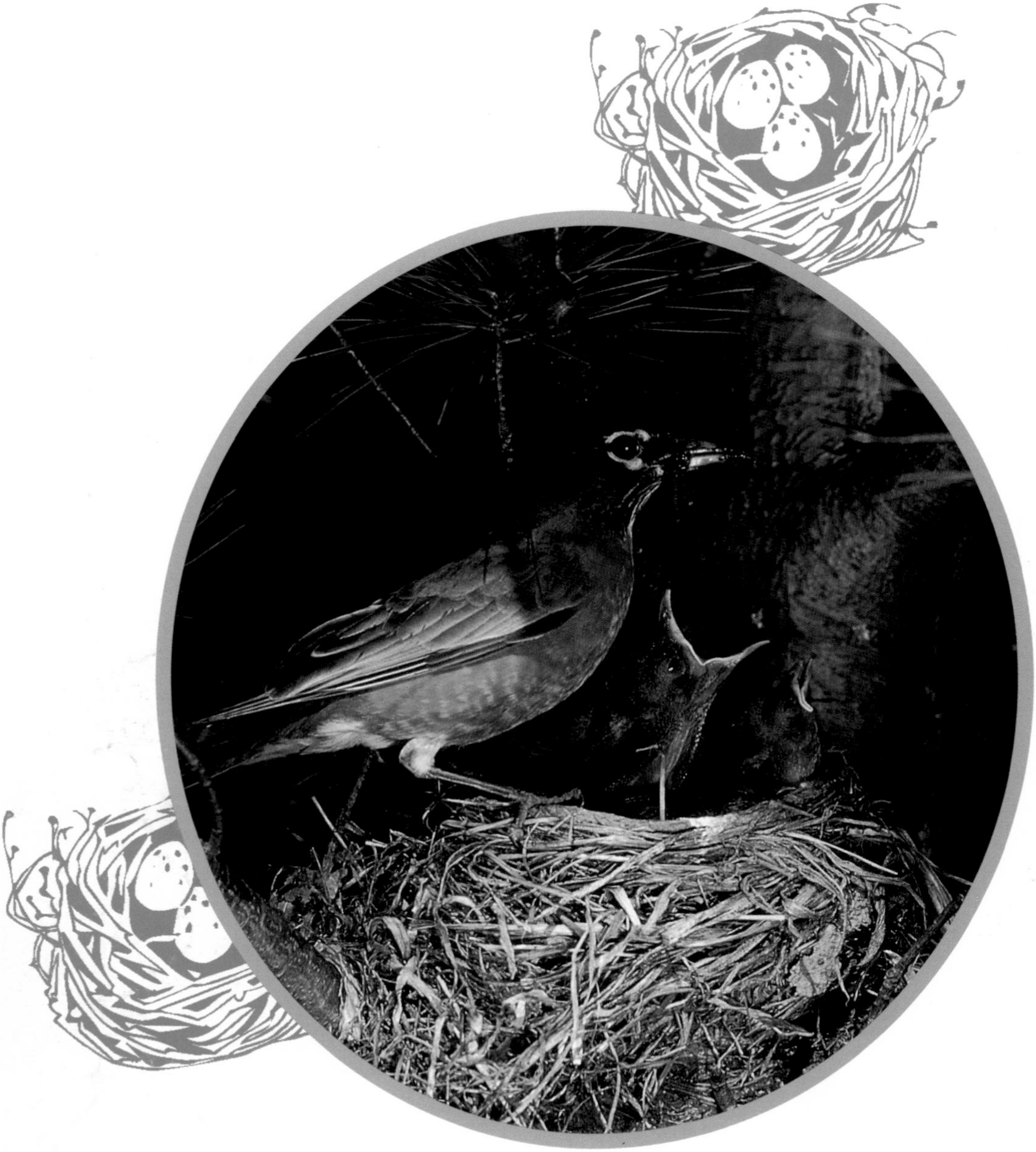

small **nest**

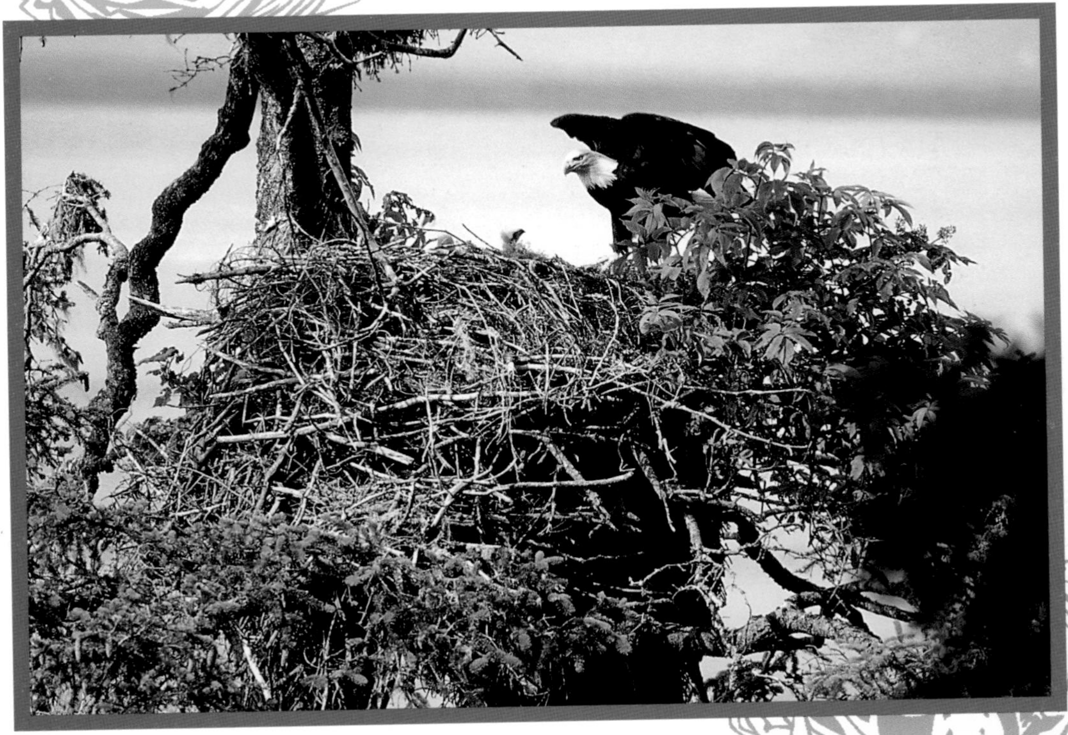

big nest

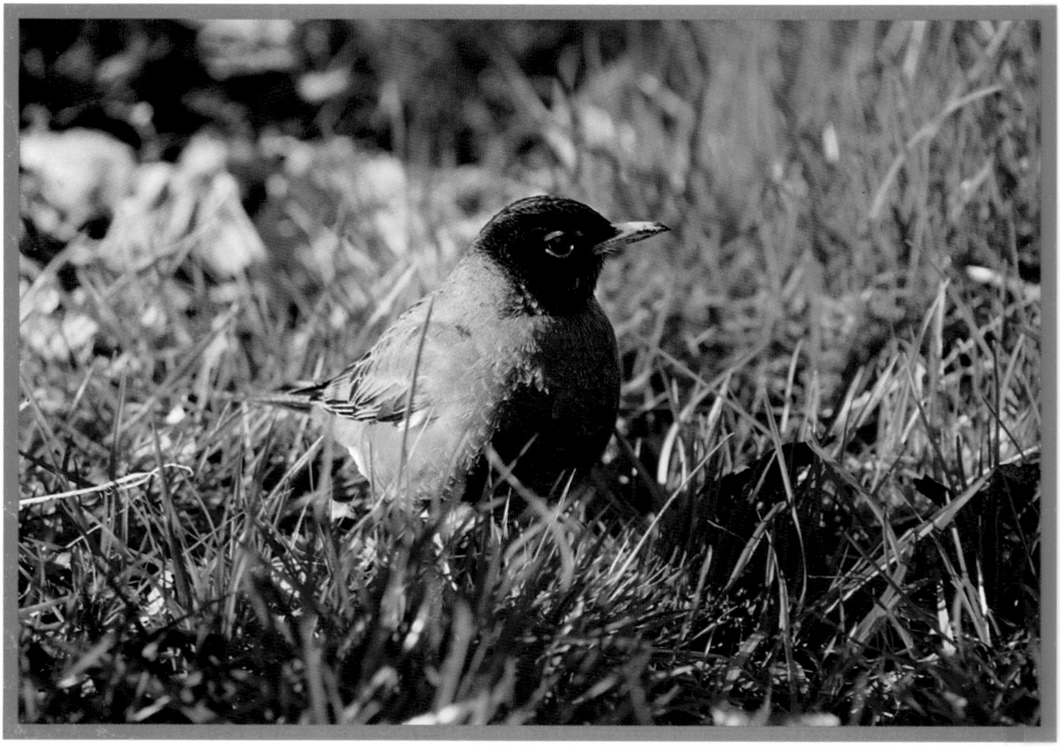

small bird

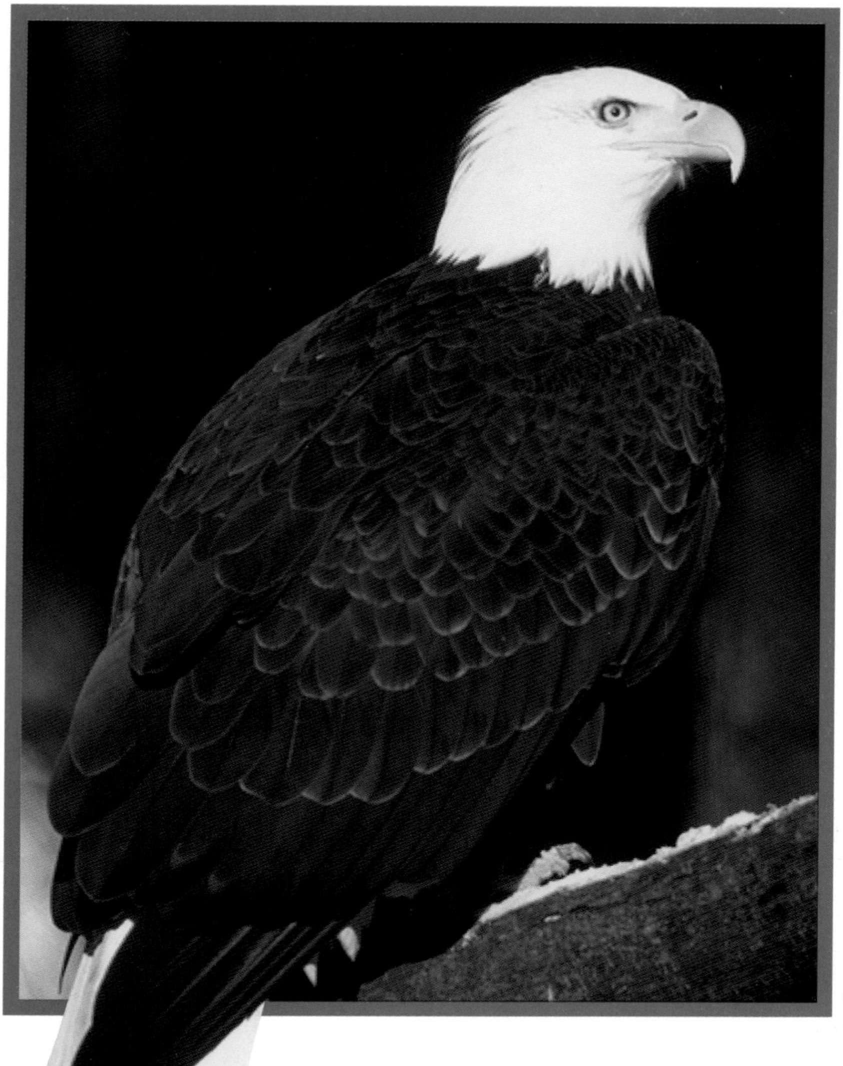

big bird

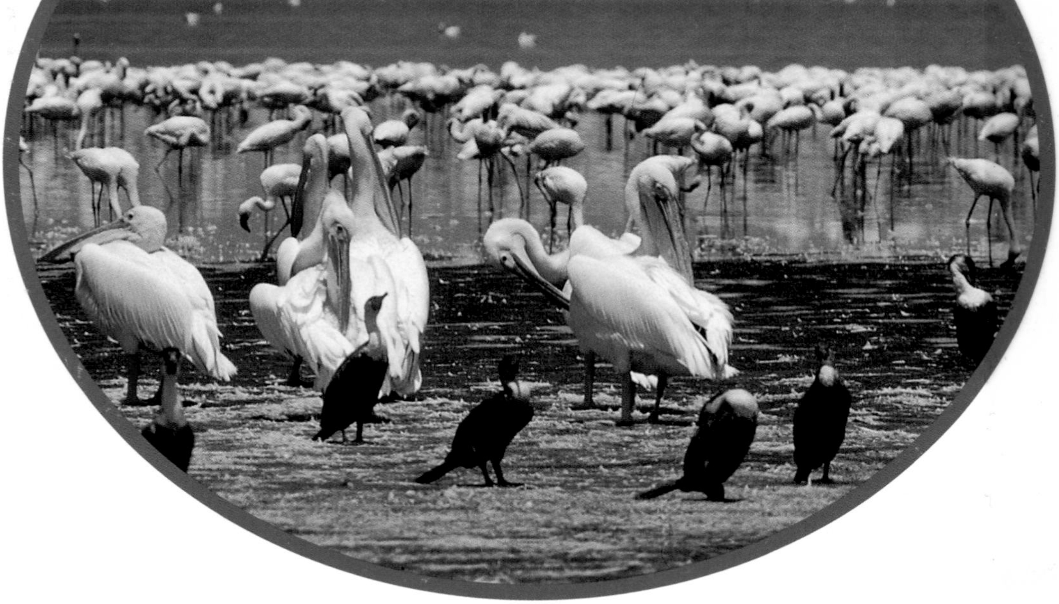

Find big birds and small birds.